THE BEST **DOGS** EVER

MINIATURE SCHNAUZERS ARE THE BEST!

Elaine Landau

LERNER PUBLICATIONS COMPANY · MINNEAPOLIS

For Christine Moesch

Lerner Publications Company
A division of Lerner Publishing Group, Inc.
241 First Avenue North
Minneapolis, MN 55401 U.S.A.

Website address: www.lernerbooks.com

Library of Congress Cataloging-in-Publication Data

Landau, Elaine.
    Miniature schnauzers are the best! / by Elaine Landau.
       p.   cm. — (The best dogs ever)
    Includes index.
    ISBN 978-1-58013-565-8 (lib. bdg. : alk. paper)
    1. Miniature schnauzer—Juvenile literature. I. Title.
    SF429.M58L36 2010
    636.755—dc22   2009015266

Manufactured in the United States of America
1 — BP — 12/15/09

TABLE OF CONTENTS

CHAPTER ONE

A GREAT FRIEND

Would you like a fun and playful friend? How about someone who is active and enjoys the outdoors? This friend would also be loyal and true.

I'm not talking about a person. I'm talking about a dog! It's a small dog with tons of spunk and style. It's a miniature schnauzer. People call it a mini schnauzer for short.

A Super Pal

Mini schnauzers make great pets. They are lively and alert. They are also smart and friendly. These outgoing pooches even seem to have a sense of humor.

Mini schnauzers are quite cute too. They have a square, stocky build and a solid, sturdy look. They weigh between 11 and 20 pounds (5 and 9 kilograms). That makes them small enough to carry.

THE NAME GAME

A great friend should have a great name. See if any of these are right for your new mini schnauzer.

Elvis   Barkie   Fluffster

Frodo   Maxine   WHISKERS

MAX

Burberry   Ralph   BaiLey

Yet mini schnauzers are more than just lap dogs. These canine cuties have lots of energy. They don't need to be carried around. They happily follow their owners about on their four sweet feet.

Two salt and pepper mini schnauzers sit near a black mini schnauzer.

Mini schnauzers come in three colors. Most are salt and pepper. That's a mix of gray and white. Others are black and silver. Still others are solid black.

A black and silver mini schnauzer stands in a field.

The Best Pooch

Mini schnauzers are hard to resist. They have bushy eyebrows and thick whiskers. Their supersweet faces can make almost anyone smile.

SHED FREE?

Some say that mini schnauzers don't shed. This isn't true. They shed a little. But they don't shed as much as most other dogs. Mini schnauzer owners don't usually find dog hair all over their clothes!

Their owners adore them. They have a dog that's both great to look at and great to be with. They think that miniature schnauzers are the best dogs ever.

A WELL-KNOWN LEADER

Former senator Bob Dole had a mini schnauzer. He named the dog Leader. Dole took the dog to meetings as well as social events. The press and public loved this cute pooch.

Leader died in 1999, but Dole and his wife, Elizabeth, stayed loyal to this great breed. They adopted another mini schnauzer. The Doles named this dog Leader II.

CHAPTER TWO

FROM THE START

Mini schnauzers have been around since the 1800s. They got their start in Germany. These dogs came about when people crossed standard schnauzers with some smaller breeds of dogs.

Standard schnauzers look just like mini schnauzers. But they're bigger! Standard schnauzers usually weigh between 30 and 50 pounds (13 and 22 kg).

DID YOU KNOW?

Standard and mini schnauzers aren't the only schnauzer varieties. Breeders also came up with a third type of schnauzer. It's called the giant schnauzer (above, right). Giant schnauzers are the biggest of the three.

Giant schnauzers are used as guard dogs. They are also used for police work. During World War II (1939–1945), these dogs even helped the U.S. Army.

Standard schnauzers were bred to be working dogs.
They helped out on farms. They herded farm animals.

Standard
schnauzers like
these were bred
to work.

Mini schnauzers were kept as
house pets. These little dogs
were good company. They were
also very helpful. They were
great at hunting rodents in their
owners' homes and barns.

Coming to the United States

Mini schnauzers came to the United States in the 1920s. These cute, friendly dogs were well liked. Farm families as well as city people wanted them. They soon became one of the United States' most popular dog breeds.

The Terrier Group

The American Kennel Club (AKC) groups dogs by breed. Some of the AKC's groups are the hound group, the toy group, and the working group. Mini schnauzers are in the terrier group.

This Afghan hound is in the hound group.

This boxer belongs to the working group.

Chihuahuas are in the toy group.

This Scottish terrier is in the same group as the miniature schnauzer.

Dogs in the terrier group do not look alike. Yet they have some things in common. These dogs are fairly small. They are also good watchdogs with lots of energy. Many people say mini schnauzers are sweeter than most terriers.

SMALL-PET SAFETY ALERT

Mini schnauzers like people. They can get along with other dogs too. Just don't put small pets such as hamsters or gerbils near them.

The mini schnauzer was bred to hunt small animals such as these. The two should never be left alone. It could be bad news for your smaller pet.

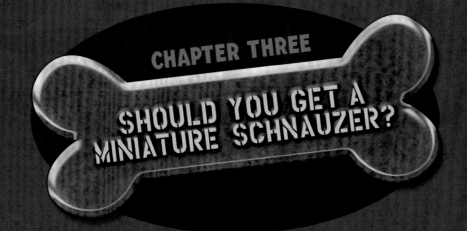

CHAPTER THREE

SHOULD YOU GET A MINIATURE SCHNAUZER?

There are lots of good reasons to get a mini schnauzer. There are also good reasons not to get one. The dog you pick should be a good match for you and your family. Read on to see if a mini schnauzer is the pet for you.

How Active Are You?

If you don't like exercise, don't get a mini schnauzer. These are active dogs. Though small, they have lots of energy.

Mini schnauzers need daily exercise. They enjoy long, brisk walks. They like to play fetch too. Some even love swimming with their owners.

Your mini schnauzer will want to work and play with you.

Do You Have Time for a Dog?

Mini schnauzers do not like being alone. They want to be with their owners. These dogs will even follow you to the bathroom!

Mini schnauzers like trips to the park. They also enjoy family picnics. They will want to go to your birthday parties as well.

Do you have time for this new best friend? If not, think about getting a goldfish instead. You don't have to spend as much time with a bird either.

AN INDOOR DOG

A mini schnauzer should never be left tied up in a yard. These dogs need to live indoors. Love and attention are important for their well-being.

Do You Want a Quiet Pet or a Watchdog?

Mini schnauzers make great watchdogs. They bark when someone comes near the house. They won't stop barking until you let them know it's okay. Some families like an alert watchdog. Others can't stand the noise. How do you and your family feel about it?

This mini schnauzer is letting its owners know that someone is nearby.

GROOMING NEEDS

Want your mini schnauzer to look great? That will take a lot of work.
These dogs have thick coats. You'll have to brush your dog daily.

Mini schnauzers also need to go to the groomer often. This can be costly.
Make sure your family can afford it.

Did you decide if a mini schnauzer is right for you? If it is, get set for lots of fun. A really great friend is about to enter your life.

Mini schnauzers are always raady for fun!

CHAPTER FOUR

COMING HOME

It's an exciting time. You're bringing home your mini schnauzer today. You've been waiting for this!

You have your camera ready. You've also told your friends about your brand-new pet-to-be. But are you really set to go? Make sure you have the supplies you'll need to care for your new pooch.

Not sure what you'll need to welcome Fido to your family? This basic list is a great place to start:

- collar

- leash

- tags (for identification)

- dog food

- food and water bowls

- crates (one for when your pet travels by car and one for it to rest in at home)

- treats (to be used in training)

- toys

PLAYTIME

Every mini schnauzer needs toys. Rubber toys are good. So are squeaky fleece toys. These dogs also love to chase after balls. You can buy dog toys at most pet stores.

Visit the Vet

You'll also want to take your dog to a veterinarian right away. That's a doctor who treats animals. They're called vets for short.

The vet will make sure your pet is healthy. Your dog will also get the shots it needs. You'll be seeing the vet again. Your dog will need more shots later on. Be sure to also take your dog to the vet if it gets sick.

A vet will help keep your mini schnauzer in good health.

Feeding Time!

Feed your pet a good-quality dog food. Ask your vet which is the best food for your dog.

Also be sure your dog has a bowl of cool, clean water. Water is as important as food for your dog. People and animals need water to live.

TRAIN YOUR DOG

Well-behaved dogs are well-trained dogs. Use love and patience in training your pup. Reward your dog with a treat for a good job.

You and Your Dog

Mini schnauzers are devoted pets. Give your mini schnauzer lots of love in return. Make it feel like part of the family. You'll have both a happy dog and a happy family.

A GOOD LIFE

Keep your pet happy and healthy. With good care, mini schnauzers live from twelve to fourteen years.

GLOSSARY

American Kennel Club (AKC): an organization that groups dogs by breed. The AKC also defines the characteristics of different breeds.

breed: a particular type of dog. Dogs of the same breed have the same body shape and general features. *Breed* can also refer to producing puppies.

breeder: someone who mates dogs to produce a particular type of dog

canine: a dog, or having to do with dogs

coat: a dog's fur

groomer: a person who cleans, brushes, and trims a dog's coat

herd: to make animals move together as a group

rodent: an animal with large, sharp front teeth that it uses for gnawing things. Miniature schnauzers were once used for hunting rodents.

shed: to lose fur

terrier group: a group of fairly small, energetic dogs. Dogs in the terrier group tend to make good watchdogs.

veterinarian: a doctor who treats animals. Veterinarians are called vets for short.

FOR MORE INFORMATION

Books

Brecke, Nicole, and Patricia M. Stockland. *Dogs You Can Draw*. Minneapolis: Millbrook Press, 2010. In this book especially for dog lovers, Brecke and Stockland show how to draw many different types of dogs.

Furstinger, Nancy. *Miniature Schnauzers*. Edina, MN: Abdo, 2006. Read this book to learn more about the smallest member of the schnauzer family. You'll also find information on how to care for this wonderful pet.

Jeffrey, Laura S. *Dogs: How to Choose and Care for a Dog*. Berkeley Heights, NJ: Enslow, 2004. This title explains where to go to pick the right dog and how to keep your pet healthy and happy.

Landau, Elaine. *Your Pet Dog*. Rev. ed. New York: Children's Press, 2007. This book is a good guide for young people on choosing and caring for a dog.

Stone, Lynn M. *Miniature Schnauzers*. Vero Beach, FL: Rourke, 2007. Learn more about the miniature schnauzer's characteristics and history in this selection.

Websites

American Kennel Club
http://www.akc.org
Visit this website to find a complete listing of AKC-registered dog breeds, including the miniature schnauzer. The site also features fun printable activities for kids.

ASPCA Animaland
http://www2.aspca.org/site/PageServer?pagename=kids_pc_home
Check out this page for helpful hints on caring for a dog and other pets.

Index

Photo Acknowledgments

The images in this book are used with the permission of: backgrounds: © iStockphoto.com/Julie Fisher and © iStockphoto.com/Tomasz Adamczyk; © iStockphoto.com/Michael Balderas, p. 1; © Elliot Westacott/Dreamstime.com, pp. 4-5, 26 (bottom), 28; © Suttisukmek/Dreamstime.com, p. 5; © Datacraft/imagenavi/Getty Images, pp. 6, 19 (top); © Wegner, P./Peter Arnold, Inc., p. 7 (top); © Jorg & Petra Wegner/Animals Animals, p. 7 (bottom); © Martin Harvey/Digital Vision/Getty Images, pp. 8 (top), 21; © Robert Pearcy/Animals Animals, p. 8 (bottom); © iStockphoto.com/Maria Bobrova, p. 9 (background); AP Photo/Ira Schwarz, p. 9 (inset); © Cheryl Ertelt/Visuals Unlimited, Inc., p. 10; © Eric Isselée/Dreamstime.com, pp. 10-11, 11; © Mary Evans Picture Library/The Image Works, p. 12 (top); © iStockphoto.com/Christopher O'Driscoll, p. 12 (bottom); © iStockphoto.com/ Deanna Quinton Larson, p. 13; © iStockphoto.com/Erie Isselée, p. 14 (top right); © Jerry Shulman/ SuperStock, p. 14 (bottom left); © Andrey Medvedev/Dreamstime.com, p. 14 (bottom right); © iStockphoto.com/Imgorthand, p. 15 (top); © Chris Brown/Alamy, p. 15 (bottom); © Jose Fajardo/ Contra Costa Times/ZUMA Press, p. 16; © Huetter, C./Arco Images GmbH/Alamy, pp. 17, 19 (bottom); © Juniors Bildarchiv/Photolibrary, p. 18; © iStockphoto.com/Daniel Rodriguez, p. 20; © Lynn Hilton/ Alamy, p. 22; © Pixbilder/Dreamstime.com, pp. 22-23; © JJM Stock Photography/Animals/Alamy, p. 23; © Aflo Foto Agency/Photolibrary, pp. 24-25 (top); © DAJ/Getty Images, pp. 24-25 (bottom); © Tammy Mcallister/Dreamstime.com, p. 26 (top); © April Turner/Dreamstime.com, p. 26 (middle); © Katie Little/Dreamstime.com, p. 27; © Clbnkbb/Dreamstime.com, p. 29 (top); © Colin Hawkins/ Stone/Getty Images, p. 29 (bottom).

Front Cover: © Value Stock Images/StockphotoPro.com.
Back Cover: © iStockphoto.com/David Palmer.